THE SOCIAL ANXIETY SOLUTION

THE PROVEN WORKBOOK FOR AN INTROVERT TO CURE SOCIAL ANXIETY DISORDER & OVERCOME SHYNESS - FOR KIDS, TEEN AND ADULTS

ED JONES

CONTENTS

WHAT TO EXPECT FROM THIS BOOK

Meeting new people is something many people find uncomfortable, but for a select few of us, it can be almost unbearable.

When you struggle with social situations to this extent, you may be suffering from a condition known as Social Anxiety Disorder.

As anyone that has suffered with this disorder will know, everyone wants to chime in with their well-meaning ideas on "tips" and "advice" to "manage" their anxiety, which, almost always turn out to be unhelpful.

Some people find solace in prescribed pills, meditation or different breathing exercises. These can all be effective, when utilized correctly, but if they're not, they can prove to be useless at best, and potentially damaging at worst.

Overcoming Social Anxiety Disorder requires a different set of strategies - counterintuitive ones. Left uncontrolled, anxiety tends to grow more and more due when a persons amygdala (the part of our brain responsible for regulating anxiety) becomes hyperactive and the situation continues to worsen.

In this book, we will uncover the science-based and counterintuitive techniques that are designed to end unwanted Social Anxiety. These methods are tried and tested, both by the author, and the thousands of people who suffered from anxiety he has helped ever since.

The goal of this book is simple:

End your Social Anxiety and shyness as quickly and as effectively as possible. In ade of that, here's a quick overview of what to expect in this book:

In Chapter 1 we'll discuss the overt signs of Social Anxiety Disorder and if this is something you may be suffering with. We'll discuss just *how common* this disorder is in today's world and the separate effects it can have on someone's life.

Chapter 2 helps us to understand the root causes of Social Anxiety Disorder. You'll get a better understanding of the different components of the disorder and what effects each of them has on people suffering from Social Anxiety Disorder and what the main symptoms are so you can understand what you're up against.

In Chapter 3 you'll discover the actual how-to steps for overcoming your Social Anxiety Disorder and how to go from someone who *suffers* from Social Anxiety Disorder, to someone who has **conquered** Social Anxiety Disorder.

Chapter 4 goes into the stage of Fully Recovering from Social Anxiety. In this chapter, we'll discuss a few of the key milestones that you will reach on your journey that will indicate you're not only on the right track, but also when you can confidently say that you have completely recovered from Social Anxiety.

In Chapter 5 you'll discover how to make powerful

resolutions to not only sustain the progress you've made, but also to overcome any lingering anxieties you may have, once and for all so you can live your life to the fullest!

Ready to get started?...Then let's go!

SOCIAL ANXIETY DISORDER

I met my friend Alex in medical school. As hard as we were working, every Saturday afternoon we found time to relax in the park with some friends and some girls. Okay, I relaxed, and the girls were all my friends. Alex found the whole thing irritating and would only do it because I was relentless in insisting he come with me. He felt like he could never even deserve a girlfriend, much less approach someone for a prospective date.

One afternoon, during one of our regular outings at the park, we noticed a pregnant woman on the floor, writhing in pain. We ran over and, stupidly, asked whether everything was okay.

• • •

Obviously, we could see she wasn't. She was gasping and asking for help in a faint voice. It became evident, pretty quickly, that she was having labor pains and we were miles away from the closest hospital. It was just Alex & I at the time—none of our other friends had arrived yet.

Everything started to move in slow motion as I felt the stress and anxiety of the situation creep up on me, but tried to focus and racked my brains for a solution. I membered there was a pharmacy just two blocks away, so I told Alex to keep an eye on her as I ran to get help.

After a breathless review of the situation, the doctors at the dispensary called a private ambulance and we were back at the park in a few short minutes.

By this time, a big crowd was circling the scene and we couldn't see what was happening. To our surprise, as we approached, we saw that Alex was holding a beautiful baby boy, wrapped up in his jacket for warmth. It was unbeliev-able! Alex had just used what he'd learned in his two years of medical school to help a woman give birth in a park! As some people took videos, others lifted Alex up on their shoulders and praised him for his brave action; however, as soon as he saw an opening, he slipped away from the crowd and the limelight of the situation. I knew he didn't like getting that kind of attention normally, but even whilst he was being praised as a hero, it was clear he still felt anxious and inadequate.

INTRODUCTION

Do you feel nervous and uncomfortable in almost every social situation? Are you afraid of being judged by others? Well, the good news is, you're not alone! Many people experience the same feeling when it comes to social occasions. The feeling is embarrassing and getting past it is important.

Even the bravest person can feel socially awkward. Perhaps it's because of the way we're brought up. Often, parents are unable to help us overcome our inner shyness. Additionally, parents may not react much when we show signs of this rampant psychological problem, as they might not understand the root causes. They might think we'll get past the "phase" as we grow older; however, the issue can get worse as time passes.

Social Anxiety can lead to a lack of confidence and a belief that you're inept in social groups, whether those involve relatives, friends, or colleagues. Within the last decade, this problem has been diagnosed as a possible root cause for various issues like depression and suicidal thoughts. This is likely linked to the fact people suffering from this problem often disengage themselves from social settings. Meeting with someone, even a close friend, can prove to be uncomfortable to people suffering from Social Anxiety. Possibly worse still, even delivering a simple presentation, one which might secure a promotion at work, can become incredibly difficult, almost impossible.

According to psychologists (and many people's personal experiences), Social Anxiety can be overcome completely. It's not nearly as bad as it seems – I promise.

This book has been written to help you fully understand what Social Anxiety Disorder is, how to cope with it, and ultimately, how to overcome it. Various forms of Social Anxiety are described in this book to help you understand what exactly you have been dealing with, so you can take the most effective course of action and overcoming your anxiety as quickly as possible.

You CAN do this. It won't always be plane sailing, but if you're willing to work at this, you can take your life back from your anxiety. Now let's get started…

THREE MAJOR COMPONENTS OF
SOCIAL ANXIETY

Often, Social Anxiety is experienced as an over-whelming feeling of fear that isn't easy to describe or control. The best way of understanding anxiety might be by breaking it into a series of components:

- *The Physical part* – what you can **FEEL**
- *The Cognitive part* – what you **THINK**
- *The Behavioral part* – what you **DO**

The Physical part

When someone becomes anxious in a social setting, a number of physical symptoms can be experienced. Things like: sweating, blushing, rambling speech, or sometimes even shaking, are not uncommon. Some of the less common, but still prominent symptoms include nausea and vomiting, a pounding heart, or shortness of breath. All of these can have a very negative impact on a person's health and well-being. When several of these symptoms present themselves at any one time, the compounded effect of the stresses can lead to panic attacks.

The Cognitive part

This component of fear refers to the types of thoughts, beliefs, presumptions, interpretations, and predictions that a person suffering from Social Anxiety can develop. Having a positive mindset is vital to fighting Social Anxiety, and we will cover a number of ways to instill this within the book. Focusing on the positives, rather than the negatives, can be a good psychological solution to Social Anxiety Disorder. As a result, the mind will avoid focusing on thoughts of danger, threats, or embarrassments and will likely alleviate many of the issues connected with Social Anxiety.

The Behavioral part

Avoiding situations is commonly the main behavioral component of Social Anxiety. People become afraid to do things, such as speaking in public and can seek to escape or avoid a social situation as a result. To ensure that they fit into various social settings, people suffering from an anxiety disorder can develop techniques to cope with their anxiety, such as wearing sunglasses to avoid eye contact, or, in some cases, having a couple of alcoholic drinks to lessen their inhibitions. Some may keep a conversation alive by asking a nonstop series of questions about the other person, just to avoid talking about themselves.

ARE YOU SUFFERING FROM GENERALIZED ANXIETY DISORDER OR SOCIAL ANXIETY DISORDER?

Generalized anxiety disorder is characterized by persistent and excessive worry about a series of things that might affect one's life. People suffering from this type of anxiety disorder may worry excessively about their health, family, career, and finances among others things. Moreover, they generally find themselves expecting the worst outcomes from future events, even when there is no justifiable reason for the concern.

People with generalized anxiety disorder tend to feel intense day-to-day stresses that others generally won't understand. Issues like; their relationship with their bosses at work or relatives at home feeling strained or fractious. Interestingly, the focus tends to be more on their ongoing relationships, rather than a fear of being judged. For example, a man with gener-alized anxiety disorder may worry *uncontrollably* about the implications of a fight with his wife. He won't even think about the blow to his ego when he apologizes first as his mind will be racing about all the terrible things that could happen if he doesn't.

Social Anxiety Disorder differs from generalized anxiety disorder, as it typically causes the person suffering from it to become much more focused on negative self-evaluations and possible rejections. Furthermore, Social Anxiety can push a person to avoid doing something for fear of being embarrassed.

IS SHYNESS THE SAME AS SOCIAL ANXIETY?

Shyness and Social Anxiety are related, but not exactly the same. The actual definitions are slightly different and the feelings associated with each are distinct.

Shyness is a tendency to be withdrawn and uncomfortable in situations involving interpersonal contact. This feeling, which can affect people at any age, can cause a person to become more of an introvert. Shy people may find it uncomfortable to maintain eye contact, and even having a quick conversation with someone can put a person on edge.

On the other hand, Social Anxiety is based on a fear of being judged by others or being embarrassed. A person may feel that what matters most is being judged by other people. It's not uncommon for shy people to develop Social Anxiety when they are forced to socialize, however, even people who are not traditionally "shy" can also suffer from Social Anxiety.

You may be suffering from Social Anxiety if you find yourself avoiding social situations for fear of being scrutinized, judged, and humiliated. A shy person who isn't suffering from Social Anxiety just avoids interacting with people.

To better illustrate the differences, here's an example:

You're supposed to be in a meeting with your colleagues, discussing the progress on a project task. All of a sudden, you start to feel that you'll be criticized at the meeting. You foresee that you might snap back to the team leader and get into a shouting match because you don't like each other. This situation is due to Social Anxiety.

Conversely, let's suppose you're on good terms with everyone on your team, but you're unexpectedly late for the meeting. You try to slip into a seat at the back of the room to stay out of the spotlight. You keep your head down and do your best to avoid eye contact, but the room turns silent and the team leader asks you to apologize to the team for keeping them waiting. You start talking in a quiet voice whilst doing your best to look anywhere but the team leader's face. You feel incredibly uncomfortable and wish you were somewhere else. This is shyness!

Just a day after the incident, Alex was on the news. They had dubbed him "the park nurse". Well, I must admit to feeling a little forgotten. Didn't anyone remember that I was there as well? Wasn't I the guy who ran across the park to get an ambulance? No one seemed interested in that. However, I reminded myself that Alex was struggling with low self-esteem that kept him from doing almost anything without me. Anywhere I went, he wanted to go too. This made me feel less envious and more understanding to Alex's struggles.

Throughout the interview segment, I did most of the talking. His voice was shaky and I was continuous that he was nervously sweating. You could tell Alex was incredibly uneasy and tried to deflect all of the questions posed to him, over to me by saying, "Maybe my friend can remember more than I can.".

The following day, a psychologist who saw the news segment called our office and introduced herself as Dr. Agnes. She congratulated us for our heroic actions and noted that she had noticed the nervousness Alex had displayed during the interview. She suggested he might be suffering with something called "Social Anxiety Disorder", a term I had never heard of before. After a brief discussion, she expressed her interest in helping Alex to overcome the disorder. She offered to help him to trace the root causes of the disorder, pinpointing behavioral patterns, discuss complications of the disorder, and counselling to help him overcome it, and she offered to do this for free after the good deed he had done!

UNDERSTANDING THE PROBLEM

I grew up in a home with my extended family. All my cousins were older, and of course, further ahead in school than I was. Often, they would laugh at me if I asked, what they considered to be, stupid questions. I remember asking my father if Jesus lived with the Care Bears in the sky. For a few days after that, my cousins couldn't stop laughing at me!

They didn't appreciate the fact that reactions to a child's inquisitiveness when growing up contributes to their mental growth in later life. Sadly, my cousins instilled a fear in me of asking stupid questions and being wrong about things. Because of this, while growing up, I rarely asked questions and I started feeling shy in front of people.

All this started from the ridicule I received from my cousins in my early life.

At school, I was the silent kid. Sometimes, I was perceived as the stupid kid as well as I didn't really participate in class. The teacher would repeatedly question whether I was paying attention as I was avoiding eye contact in fear of being asked questions and having to talk in front of the class.

Symptoms of anxiety disorder

The most common sign of Social Anxiety Disorder is shyness or discomfort in certain situations. Comfort levels vary depending on personality traits, life experiences, and the setting of the situation itself. Some people tend to be naturally reserved, while others are more outgoing. Social Anxiety Disorder mainly starts to manifest itself in younger children and teenagers, but it can sometimes start in adults.

Some of the major signs that a person may be suffering from the disorder are:

Emotional and behavioral symptoms

- Fear of situations in which you're prone to being judged by people
- Excessive concern about embarrassing or humiliating yourself
- Intense phobia of meeting, interacting, or talking with acquaintances or strangers
- Fear that people will notice that you look anxious
- Fear of physical symptoms that may be embarrassing, such as: sweating, blushing, trembling or having a shaky voice
- Avoiding speaking to people out of fear of being misquoted or misunderstood
- Avoiding situations where you will be the center of attention
- Feeling nervous about an activity or event in the near future
- Tolerating a social situation with deep fear or anxiety
- Taking time after a social situation to identify mistakes in your conversations and analyze your overall social performance
- Anticipating the worst possible consequences from a negative experience
- Experiencing intense fear and anxiety during public speaking or performing in public (stage fright)

- For children, anxiety may be shown by crying, temper tantrums, clinging to parents in the presence of a stranger, or refusing to speak in social situations.

Physical symptoms

Physical symptoms that may sometimes accompany Social Anxiety Disorder include:

- Blushing
- The inability to maintain eye contact when conversing
- Pounding heartbeat
- Whole-body trembling
- Sweating on the face or on palms
- Developing an upset stomach or nausea
- Having trouble catching your breath
- Dizziness or lightheadedness
- Feeling that your mind has gone blank
- Muscle tension, usually manifested as a stiff neck

Avoiding common social situations

Day-to-day occurrences that people suffering from Social Anxiety might struggle with include: may be hard to endure when you have Social Anxiety Disorder include:

- Being in the presence of unfamiliar people or strangers
- Going to work or school
- Making eye contact while speaking
- Dating & flirting
- Attending parties or social gatherings (weddings, the movies, a party)
- Returning items to a store
- Entering a room where people are already settled
- Eating and drinking in front of others
- Using a public bathroom

Social Anxiety symptoms can change over time. Fears can flare up if a person is facing additional stress or demands. Avoiding situations that produce anxiety may feel helpful in the short-term; however, your anxiety is likely to continue or even worsen over the long-term if you don't treat or learn how to effectively manage it.

WHAT CAUSES SOCIAL ANXIETY DISORDER?

The underlying causes of Social Anxiety are complex and tend to vary from one person to another. Given this, it's difficult to generalize the causes of this disorder across different people. Anecdotally, the majority of sufferers seem to develop this condition out of a fear of being judged or even humiliated. Others may be excessively worried about tomorrow and what it could bring. For everyone, the root cause can be different, but the outcome is the same: it's unpleasant at best and utterly debilitating at worse.

Despite the complexity that characterizes Social Anxiety, researchers have tried demystifying the major causes. The following are some of the most viable causes of the disorder:

The brain

According to researchers, specific parts of the brain may have a role to play in the development of Social Anxiety. Based on the findings of recent research, certain parts of the brain are more active than others when a person is experiencing Social Anxiety.

What researchers term as: "Having an overactive amygdala" (the part of the brain that controls the fear response), may be the main cause of Social Anxiety.

When there is muted synchronization between parts of their brain, a person can become unsettled and, therefore, becomes anxious and can develop negative thought patterns and internal judgments.

Irregularities in the way chemical messengers that transmit information from one brain cell to another, may have a role to play in causing Social Anxiety.

Diagnosis and treatment of any type of anxiety can be difficult, with current, conventional treatments that aren't always effective.

Genetics

Social Anxiety can be a family problem. If one parent

or grandparent was afflicted with Social Anxiety Disorder, the next generation can be more likely to experience the same fate. A person whose parents are sufferers of Social Anxiety can be up to ten times more prone to suffering from the disorder. This is a pretty solid indication that Social Anxiety can be inheritable from one generation to the next.

Some people discard the notion of inherited mental disorders and, whilst it may be true that an individual may be different from the rest of a family, possible genetic predisposition to anxiety and other disorders can't be ignored.

Negative life experiences

When someone experiences a difficult or even dehumanizing event, the likelihood of developing anxiety or other mental illness can increase. Studies have shown that people who endure difficult circumstances during childhood are among the biggest sufferers of the disorder. Women who are raped when they are young may always fear interacting with men as a results. Incidents like this can lead to farther-reaching effects, like women developing an irrational fear or anxiety response when interacting with male members of their family.

Early Social Interaction

Growing up amid shy people may contribute to a person acquiring the same traits. This is because, as we grow, we have a propensity to learn how to behave by watching others and imitating them. If you take a moment to analyse your mannerisms, beliefs & daily actions, you may find these mirror your parents or friends whilst growing up.

In addition, close friends and relatives can sometimes make comments about our behaviors that can influence us, based upon how they perceive us. We may draw negative conclusions about their concerns and begin thinking about how to correct our supposed "negative" behavioral patterns. Consequently, we can develop fears and anxieties because of them. We find it increasingly difficult to face these people since we only focus on the negative side of their comments and therefore, we learn to avoid those people and situations, and this can lead to avoid meeting or having a conversation with anyone.

Internal Beliefs

People who mistakenly view social situations as dangerous or life-threatening are most likely to feel uncomfortable. Anxiety causes a person to feel that they must always impress others. They might think that the other person has a weird perception of them.

In order to eliminate this feeling, it's important to disengage the mind from that mentality and change it, for the better.

Sadly, negative beliefs can also cause a person to have a negative impression of others. Once you believe that someone is bad, you can be hard-pressed to start believing they are anything but bad. Stopping beliefs from ruining your life is a simple thing, in theory - just stop believing something is true, but in practice, it can be much more challenging.

Behaviors

Behaviors are unconscious processes that can be very difficult to uproot and change. (Unintentionally) making shyness a habit will obviously lead to Social Anxiety. Moreover, if you become a person who hates social gatherings, won't ever start a conversation with a stranger, or meet someone new, which, obviously, can have some seriously negative impacts on your personally and professional life.

It's important to be conscious of and try to avoid such behaviors. They don't help in any way and just add up to the many problems that we already have in life, so think positive!

HOW CAN SOCIAL ANXIETY DISORDER AFFECT YOUR LIFE?

Social Anxiety can seriously affect a person's life. Routine social interactions like meeting friends, strangers, or even simple things like eating in front of people can cause extreme stress and anxiety.

This anxiety can even cause someone to miss out on important chances in their life. For example, imagine being qualified and ready to start your dream job. You've submitted your resume and you've been called in for an interview...but now you're paralyzed with the fear of meeting the interviewer. You start to run through all the terrible things that could happen and you get even more worked up. You decide the only way to avoid all that potential pain is to call off the interview.

Now you've missed out on your dream job and all

the amazing opportunities it could have brought you because your Social Anxiety got the better of you. It's a sad state of affairs, but it's someone people struggle with every day.

Composure and courage are the only way to overcome these issues and you must act NOW, before it ruins your life.

Without appropriate treatment, Social Anxiety Disorder can persist throughout a person's life. Certain fears that start off as trivial issues can end up dominating a person's life choices. This can interfere with daily life, schooling, career, relationships, and their general happiness.

First things first - A word on Suicidal thoughts or suicide attempts

One of the most horrendous and inconceivably sad parts of modern life is that more and more people are choosing to take their own life. Young men especially seem to be at risk with 40-60% of all suicide attempts carried out my men.

Anxiety is capable of making life feel utterly unbearable, believe me I know, I've been there - and it's not fun. It can feel like taking your own life is the only answer to end the pain and bleakness. It sounds like a simple fix to a complex problem. It's a way to end the misery and the pain felt on a daily-basis. However, and this is a BIG however, Social Anxiety, depression or any other disorder you may be saddled with IS SOMETHING THAT CAN BE SUCCESSFULLY DEALT WITH! I wrote that all in caps because it's so important. If you are having thoughts of suicide, please, PLEASE call someone who knows what they're doing and they can at least give you some personalised guidance as to how to start coping, and ultimately overcome the issues you're struggling with.

If you're in the US, you can call the USA National Suicide Hotline on: *1-800-SUICIDE : 1-800-784-2433* or on: *1-800-273-TALK : 1-800-273-8255*

If you're in the UK, you can call the Samaritans, 24 hours a day, 7 days per week on: 116 123

If you're in a different country, just Google "suicide hotline" and you'll be given a local number to you.

Please don't let fear or embarrassment stop you, these people are trained, they do this day in, day out and they do it because they want to help people, just like you!

Now that's out of the way, let's look at some of the other ways of Social Anxiety affects people's lives:

Low self-esteem

People with low self-esteem tend find failure exceptionally difficult. They have a high propensity to internally exaggerate negative experiences. A person may take an off-the-cuff comment from someone as a personal attack on their character. Because of this, they find themselves even more likely to have low self esteem. This vicious cycle repeats itself until they fear social interaction of any kind.

ALCOHOLISM AND SUBSTANCE ABUSE

For some sufferers of Social Anxiety Disorder, a history of alcohol or substance-abuse may be a factor in the onset of the disorder.

Maybe you know someone, a friend or family member, who like to have a drink...a little too often. On the days they are sober they never want to talk to anyone about anything. They lives isolated and rarely make time to even share a meal.

This person is a victim of Social Anxiety. They drink to gain the courage to face people or to start a conversation, and the whole process repeats itself.

It's not uncommon for a lot of people have a drink or two before (and during) attending a social event. They mask their fears with drunkenness. It's as if they draw courage from alcohol and will feel out of place if they stop drinking.

Others take various drugs to get the same results, taking a few puffs of a joint or a few lines of cocaine to help them feel "more sociable", when really, they are just masking their own insecurities.

Eventually, these people can become substance abusers. It's incredibly unfortunate that they now have a second problem to fight.

A lot of time, effort and money is spent on rehabilitation every year, and sadly, not everyone can be helped. Some people who drink or use drugs recreationally to mask their fears become lifetime addicts, perhaps falling into a cycle where they leave the drug they relied on, only to relapse at a later stage, potentially cause by the stress of those same social interactions they had first sought solace from.

Less productivity at work

Social Anxiety leads you to feel awkward among your colleagues so you tend to avoid activities that involve teamwork. This, of course, affects your working relationships and can actually lead to people having a negative opinion of you because you are so withdrawn.

When you're at work, you may find you take a lot of time on a particular task since you think your results are not good enough and might be rejected by your boss, so you work harder and longer at your work to gain their approval.

It can get very rough for a person suffering with Social Anxiety to hit deadlines. As a result, they may find themselves at risk of losing their job or career if they are not able to "connect" with the team.

Hypersensitivity to criticism

Hypersensitivity tends to manifest itself as an extreme fear being judged by others, by being embarrassed, or humiliated. To a certain extent, this is normal, however, getting irate when others offer constructive criticism on actions is not. Life is full of lessons, and being criticized is one of the many chances a person gets to learn. Unfortunately, Social Anxiety can make a person think that other people don't recognize their efforts and may well disregard the fact their criticism may help them improve their performance and/or situation.

Isolation and difficult social relationships

Most victims of Social Anxiety Disorder have a tendency to isolate themselves. Rarely do they make friends. Remembering that humans are social creatures, and living alone tends to lead to loneliness, this can be an issue.

Making moves toward a person of the opposite sex also proves to be easier said than done. In fact, many people suffering with Social Anxiety Disorder never enter any sort of romantic relationship, let out a lasting one. There are often a series of disconnects in discussions and sufferers may feel (wrongly) that their partner isn't serious about the relationship.

Negative self-talk

From time to time, we find ourselves thinking about how "I should have said *this*.", or "I wish I hadn't of done *that*.", then cursing ourselves and reinforcing a belief that we're stupid or worthless. This can be down to a simple failure to achieve a goal or when we make a mistake at home, school or at work. We continually call ourselves names and , at times, we even list things we're not good at. We don't believe in our potential.

Low academic achievement

For students, anxiety can be particularly all-consuming. Anxiety can cause a student to feel uncomfortable asking or answering questions in class; therefore, the process of learning is curtailed. During exams, some students develop sweaty hands where even holding a pen becomes problematic.

If it makes you feel any better, even Eminem suffered with it:

"His palms are sweaty, knees weak, arms are heavy."

Trouble being assertive

Assertiveness is one of the most universally agreed-upon personality traits that is almost directly correlated with success in a person's life.

People suffering from Social Anxiety Disorder may find themselves unable to stick with any decision. When pressured by others, they may find themselves changing their stance on anything as they feel unable to stand up for themselves, or their beliefs. Being assertive helps a person to stick to what they believe in and, ultimately, have less regrets in the future. Not being assertive can have serious negative consequences down the line, not only in a professional sense, but in personal relationships as well.

Without a solid sense of self and rigidness in their beliefs, a person my find themselves with lifelong regrets, feeling that they had always failed to make the right choice.

Sometimes, people who should encourage us to be brave and face Social Anxiety Disorder are doing what the feel is in out best interests, but they just don't know how to help in the most effective way.

I remember my mother trying to advise me on how to overcome my Social Anxiety, but, despite having her best interest at heart, her suggestions where just appealing and, perhaps even worse, they were not effective either!

The turning point for me was in fourth grade. My teacher had noticed I was less than eager to participate and practically froze on the spot when asked to "come to the front of the class". After confirming with my mother and I, she begun giving me counseling sessions to help me through my struggle. She was the first person I learned about the concept of Social Anxiety Disorder from. She introduced me to books which had solutions. Gradually, I started practicing the steps I read about and, after a series of sessions with my teacher and a lot of hard work from my end, I can very confidently say I no longer suffer with Social Anxiety, in fact, I'm usually the most talkative person in any given group!

Remember Dr Agnes? Well, she was the second person that I heard talking about the disorder from a knowledgeable perspective. This time, I took notes and vowed to share this information with as many people as I could to help them overcome their own struggles with Social Anxiety Disorder.

I worked 1 on 1 with people in my local area at first, then I reached out through social media to people from all over the globe who were struggling. I found I had developed a keen interest in helping people overcome their problems and so, I decided to study the problem in more detail, take what was working from the approaches people were using and combine my findings to write this book.

It's my sincere hope this book can help you to conquer your fears and anxieties and to take your life back!

ENDING THE ANXIETY PROBLEM

*W*hen you develop Social Anxiety, public speaking is a major problem. Public speaking is a hard thing and can make some people completely freeze up while on stage. Recently, I was part of an annual general meeting of shareholders at one of the largest real estate companies in the country. There were specialists from each department of the company presenting their annual reports, however, there was one particular lady who stands out in my memory. She was well presented, probably in her early-thirties with a smart dress and sensible shoes on. As she tottered on to the stage with her shoulders rolled forward and her eyes to the ground, you could tell this was not something she was comfortable with.

. . .

For a moment, it looked like my fears of her fear was unfounded as she quite loudly and confidently said "Good morning!" to the waiting crowd, and then...silence. She just stood there like she'd forgotten what she walked in the room for.

From where I was seated, I could see her hands were shaking terribly. She was in the middle of an Anxiety attack and her mind has gone blank. I recognised it because I've experienced the same thing, on a number of occasions.

She managed to splutter out the first couple of words of her prepared presentation and tried to gain some momentum, but even after just five minutes, she was visibly wheezing due to her hyperventilating the entire time. She managed to limp through the rest of her presentation without fainting but made a very swift exit from the stage as soon as she had closed the last slide.

Her reaction is understandable when you think about a famous quote from Mr. Seinfeld:

• • •

"According to most studies, people's number one fear is public speaking. Number two is death. Death is number two. Does that sound right? This means to the average person, if you go to a funeral, you're better off in the casket than doing the eulogy."

MANAGING SOCIAL ANXIETY DISORDER

The main purpose of this book is to help you over-come Social Anxiety Disorder. The content in this section aims to present you with the best possible solutions to reduce and ultimately end the problem you're suffering with.

Lowering Social Anxiety can be hard in the begin-ning stages; however, it does become easier over time. Below are some of the most effective ways to help any person, at any age start to get a grip on their Social Anxiety.

Consult a therapist

Social Anxiety Disorder can be extremely hard to deal with at an individual level. If you find yourself in this situation, you should seek the help of a psychologist as early as possible. It's prudent to find a therapist who specializes in anxiety disorders, but not essential as all professional psychologists receive training on anxiety relief for patients.

Going through therapy or a counseling program with a specialist will help reframe your perceptions. By sharing your feelings with a confidante, you will reinforce the healing process and it's a way of showing yourself that you acknowledge you have a problem and need help. During the therapy sessions, make sure you discuss all the situations that make you feel anxious and the psychologist will be able to give you personalised, professional advise on how to reframe and overcome your anxiety and fears.

Think positively prior to social events

Working out a routine to calm yourself before a social event can help you gain composure as much as it can relieve your mind. Activities that make you feel happy can help in releasing "feel-good" chemicals in the brain. Eventually, this relaxes the brain and will aid in overcoming stressful encounters. Things like: listening to your favorite music, watching a movie, or playing a video game may be helpful to put you into a relaxed and positive state of mind before heading out to a social event.

Switch off the negative thoughts

Your imagination is a wonderful thing. If utilized constructively, it can be of massive benefit; however, using your imagination to scare yourself is more dangerous than it sounds. It sounds pretty harmless in isolation, but recurring negative thoughts can quickly ingrain themselves into your subconscious.

This negative thought pattern seems to pop up most often when someone is trying to imagine what other people think and feel about them. Usually, it starts off on a negative note and gets worse from there. These kind of thoughts are not helpful! No one can read other people's thoughts (despite what might be claimed by certain performers), so trying to infer what someone feels about you is not only a waste of your time, but you'll likely make any future interactions with them awkward as you'll be second-guessing what they are saying as you'll "know" what they "really" think about you.

This holds true when making a public presentation also. Don't worry about if people will judge your delivery style. You just do You. Imagine them in their underwear (if that's your thing), but you don't have to feel intimidated by them. You can stand in front of a crowd and talk to them, freely and easily - you just have to believe you can. Trying to figure out what people's perceptions of you are from the looks on their faces is a time-wasting and strenuous process. It will hamper your presentation so switching off such thoughts is helpful (although, not easy at first). Ultimately, we can influence the way people may think about us by becoming more socially confident and composed, so remember: *F**K what they think, and they'll love you for it!*

Exercise

There are very few things in this world that are as effective as raising someone's mood and confidence as exercise. I'm not saying you have to train like you're inthe Olympics, and you don't have to sweat until your clothes stink.

You can do small interval workout (HIIT) that take less than 10 minutes, or a light walk or jog for however long you feel like. The point is to find something you enjoy (or at the very least, don't actively lothe). If you exercise regularly, say three times a week, you're less likely to feel anxious on some occasions.

And hey, if you lose a bit of belly fat and start seeing that 6-pack poke through, you're going to feel more confident as well, right?

Spend time outdoors

Relaxing in the open air alone or with other people can also be helpful in fighting Social Anxiety & depression. Humans have spent the past few million years surrounded by nature, and it's only in the last couple of hundred years we've moved into increasingly more dense and overpopulated cities. Getting outside and back to nature can go a long way in boosting a person's relaxation. Numerous studies have shown the health benefits like: Lowering your blood pressure, relieving muscle tension and reducing stress hormones - all factors which are known to accelerate Social Anxiety Disorder.

Having a relaxing moment outdoors doesn't have to take all day. Just grab a few minutes at lunch or in the morning in your backyard, a local park, wood or lake (if you're lucky enough to live near one). 5-10 minutes can be enough to see some real benefits and feel more centered. You may notice you're calmer and more confident as you go through your day if you start it was a relaxing stroll through nature...

Meditation

Meditation has had something of a revival in recent years, so I guess it's not really necessary to answer in detail some of the common objections that usually crop up:

1. "Isn't it all woo-woo nonsense?"
2. "I don't want to be a monk, thank you very much."
3. "I feel stupid."
4. "I've tried it before and my mind wouldn't go quiet.".

To which I would say:

1. No, countless variations of meditation have been studied even just in the past decade, and the results are unanimously positive. Meditation is science-backed and *it works*.
2. Religion and spirituality doesn't have to have anything to do with meditation, unless you want it too.
3. Everyone does, but the secret it, no one cares if you're sat there chanting "oommmmmm" to yourself. They'll probably want in on it once they see the

amazing benefits you get from the practice.

4. Meditation is definitely a skill that One has to acquire (why do you there the monks are still at it all day, every day?), but the good news is, you can learn the basics and get good-enough to feel some serious benefits from the practice from your *first* session.

Meditation is a great way to help you relax your mind. It helps to focus on the present by following your breathing. This keeps the mind free of all thoughts, including the negative ones. Once the mind has taken a break and calmed down, the natural propensity is to focus on the positive, so you might find more positive thoughts come more naturally when you start practicing meditation.

The fun part is that meditation is a great tool to reframe thoughts and look at them from a different perspective. You might find those "big worries" are a little less significant once you've viewed them from a few different angles.

If you want to get started with meditation or at least give it a *try* I would suggest starting with a meditation app like *Headspace* or *Calm*. Both are free to download and try so you don't have to shell out any cash to see if meditation is for you. All you need is a smart phone (or computer) and a pair of headphones. Now go and grab the app, what are you waiting for!?

Practice yoga

Yoga is often referred to a a form of meditation. Manoeuvring the body in certain positions can strengthen and stretch the muscles and other body tissues. Consciously practicing Yoga moves helps to disengage the mind from anything but the here and now (and that includes disengaging from your worries). At the same time, calm, rhythmic breathing can effectively lower your heart rate and blood pressure to help you become less anxious long after you have finished the Yoga session.

I appreciate that Yoga isn't going to be everyone's cup of tea, do feel free to skip this one and focus on meditation instead, but if it does sound like something you'd like to try, you can start off by following YouTube videos and work your way up to participating in a class with others once you feel up to it.

Aromatherapy

Heating certain natural herbs and plant extracts has

been a proven remedy for stress and anxiety for hundreds of years. Simple scents, such as lavender, chamomile, and rosewater, are a great starting point if you are interested in trying out aromatherapy. You'll find concentrated oils of each of these readily available online. These oils produce a wonderful smell when heated and have no harmful effects on the body. You can also rub the sap of the plants on the skin (if you're not allergic, of course). Scientists say that sweet scents can influence the functionality of the brain, positively affecting moods, and emotions. Aromatherapy is definitely something to try if you're more of an "indoor" person (myself included).

Get a massage

Alright, so this one is a little indulgent, but bear with me.

Feeling a therapist's expert hands work the tension out of your muscles can really help to calm you. Reflexology is done by rubbing, squeezing, and pressing into areas with a lot of tension to help release it. As well as relaxing the muscles, it helps to relax you and, in effect, lessen your anxiety.

It's not necessarily the cheapest option on this list,

but it's probably the most pleasant!

Limit alcohol intake

Drinking a few bottles of beer may seem relaxing but when you remember alcohol affects your brain in its ability to process information & make decisions, it starts to sound like a bad idea.

Drinking regularly and heavily can cause a person to be indecisive at times and they may feel that others are being judgmental about their drinking - which may be true.

Alcoholism affects a person's overall health, which is why consistently, doctors advise against a high alcohol intake because it leads to liver problems, among other things.

Drinking to mask Social Anxiety is a short-term fix and can cause more harm than good, so if you find yourself drinking to lessen your anxiety, try to lower the volume for a short time and work through the other steps in this book.

Join support groups

Sufferers of Social Anxiety Disorder can find it difficult to join support groups due to their antisocial tendencies; however, such groups can be incredibly helpful as they are full of people with similar problems. In such groups, participants aren't concerned with judging others, they are there to help themselves and other members of the group and to provide a safe space so everyone can feel comfortable.

When joining a group, you will be encouraged to share your troubles honestly and openly. This will feel uncomfortable at first, but once you are accustomed to the group and feel comfortable with the people around you, you will find it much easier to open up and let them help with suggestions and solutions.

In a support group of people suffering with Social Anxiety Disorder, unbiased and candid opinions are shared concerning each individual's problems, and how to manage them. Not only does this provide a real-world example of the old saying: *"a problem shared, is a problem halved"*, but you may well see that other people struggling with the disorder have a harder time of it than you.

By disclosing your experiences in such groups, you

will learn first-hand, that thoughts regarding judgment and rejection are distorted and untrue. Most importantly, you will learn how others with a similar problem approach and overcome fears of social situations.

Sleep Better

Sleeping is an incredible, natural and free solution for a number of psychological problems. In fact, doctors are advocates for lengthy and quality sleeping periods as a way to deal with stress and depression.

Ensuring you are getting enough sleep ensures your body and brain have time to relax and recharge to help you deal with the day ahead. Getting enough quality sleep also has a mood-boosting effect all of it's own, and you'll find yourself better able to focus on what you're doing at any given time.

As a general recommendation, aiming for 8-9 hours of SLEEP per night seems to have the most beneficial effects. Sleep is in all-caps because that's what's needed - SLEEP, not watching TV in bed or scrolling through social media.

Block out the time and commit to getting at least 8 hours of SLEEP for at least 1 week, and then see how you feel. If you find it's not improving your life (unlikely!), then you can go back to binge-watching Netflix until 2AM, but if you do notice a positive difference (much more likely!), then I encourage you to prioritise getting high-quality and a high-quantity of sleep on a regular-basis to help overcome your anxiety issues.

Ask others about yourself

Isolating yourself and spending time pondering your mishaps and mistakes is not a very effective way to make yourself feel better. If you want to know yourself better, then ask the people around you how they perceive you. It's important to stress to them that they need to give credit where it's due, but also that lying won't help you get any better. Constructive criticism is what is required and they should support you in working to better yourself.

You can help with this by cultivating curiosity. By asking people questions that require simple "yes" or "no" answers, you will be stopping the conversation short. Instead, focus on asking people to expand on their thoughts and answers. Asking questions like: *"That's a really interesting point, could you tell me a little more about it?"* and *"I agree completely. Just out of interest, how did you arrive at that conclusion?"*.

As a general rule, people love to talk about themselves and their thoughts (even if those thoughts are about you), so you'll find this exercise naturally endears people to you, so you'll be having more positive interactions with people in a completely natural way.

You also need to bear in mind that, at times, people may criticize certain behaviors that appear antisocial, shy, or egotistical. It's important to try to view this criticism positively as this is someone genuinely trying to help you. Make a promise to yourself to gradually take any good advice on board and implement it in your life, where possible.

Catching up with people a few days or weeks later to tell them how their advice has positively impacted your life will make their day!

Try Biofeedback Therapy

Biofeedback therapy works by using technology to show you, in real-time, how your body is responding. Using this feedback, you're able to see what actions and thought-processes boost relaxation and relieve anxiety, and also to identify what triggers these negative states in the first place.

This can be a costly therapy and may not be readily available where you are, however, it's a proven technique that works to pinpoint the various situations which make a person feel uncomfortable.

There are various "levels" of biofeedback therapy, ranging from measuring your heart rate, or heart rate variability (HRV) with your phone camera or Bluetooth chest strap, that help you to infer a stress response from the data, all the way up to having electrodes placed on your head and chest to get real-time, multi-channel feedback from your body.

The major role of these electrodes is to send signals or pulses to a screen where you and the therapist can read and interpret them. Mainly, the therapist will ask the patient questions about situations that make them nervous. Patients will exhibit physical symptoms which are translated by the computer through the sensors. The sensors monitor the patient's heartbeat pattern, breathing rate, blood pressure, muscle activity, and skin temperature.

Through this therapy, a person can determine the particular situations that make them feel anxious or agitated. A biofeedback therapist can help you practice relaxation exercises after reviewing your results. Within a short period, this can help you control your anxiety, and lead to completely curing it eventually.

F**K Gossip

Constantly worrying about who is gossiping about you is stressful. Why would you care anyway? Practice becoming used to people talking (and potentially talking about you). Acknowledge that you can never be everyone's favorite person and being constantly concerned about what people might be saying about you is guaranteed to make you feel anxious, so be mindful of when you feel these thoughts pop up and re-focus on the positives of the interaction.

Set reasonable priorities

Having a purpose and taking concrete action towards it are sure-fire ways to promote fulfillment and happiness. This can be as simple as coming up with a to-do list of prioritized goals and starting work on your Most Important Task (MIT). This will help you figure out what needs immediate action, and what can wait.

This will also teach you self-discipline so you don't miss out on, or postpone any goal.

The simplest way to achieve any goal is to work methodically on each MIT until it's complete and then start on the next one. This avoids jumping from goal to goal or task to task unnecessarily.

Make sure to set achievable goals that can be attained within a realistic timeframe.

Setting your sights on becoming a millionaire by tomorrow is, maybe, not so likely to happen, but setting a goal and an solid, well-defined action plan towards becoming financially free within the next 3-5 years - now *that* is doable.

Ask for help, if necessary, and don't worry about things that are not important to your goals. Try to avoid discrediting your achievements or focusing on the negatives if a goal is not met by your self-defined time frame. Any goal not met is simply an opportunity to learn from it and become a better person.

Even as you set goals for things that need to be done to make your life better (finances/health/fitness etc.), try to incorporate objective *behavioral* goals. These will help you fight your fears and overcome Social Anxiety Disorder. For example, setting a goal to meet 3 new people and start conversations in the next week might sound like hell on earth, but if you set this as a goal and push yourself to achieve it, by the end of the week you'll look back at what you've achieved and realize you've massively expanded your comfort zone!

List all of your achievements

A simple and easy way to avoid focusing on the negative self-talk is to put together a list of all of the things you are proud of. Writing out and referring to, this list makes you feel that, whilst you can't be good at everything, you have some positive achievements in your life that you can smile about.

You can start by writing 1 or 2 things you have achieved, no matter how small they may appear to you, that you can look back on and smile about. Take some time and reflect on all the hard work you have put in to arrive at your current position. This way, you will own and embrace your achievements and create a great foundation for eliminating anxiety with a positive mindset.

Have a positive response to failure and mistakes

To make errors is to be human. Cursing yourself because of a mistake doesn't do you any favors, but it's an all too common issue for almost everyone, not just people suffering with Social Anxiety.

Instead of cursing yourself about the mistake that was made, consciously encourage yourself by believing that you learnt something from the experience and now you will know better for next time.

Renowned Ford Motor Company founder Henry Ford said that *"failure is the only opportunity to begin again more intelligently."*

Sitting alone and thinking about other people's perceptions of your mistakes is common, but again, not very helpful to you or your Anxiety levels. You can never know what's on another person's mind, so don't waste time judging yourself. Focus on the next step to achieving one of your goals and get back into that positive mindset.

Practice doing what makes you anxious

Otherwise known as *"inoculation therapy"*, this strategy involves slowly introducing yourself to the things that make you feel anxious in a bid to lessen the negative feelings over time.

Dare yourself! Identify the situations that make you

anxious and create a list, ranking your fears from least to worst. With this list, you'll be ready to confront your fears (little by little).

Let's say your biggest fear is talking to a member of the opposite sex (for brevity, we'll use approaching women as the example).

In this instance, you would break down the fear into steps leading up to it. For example, on day 1, you could set yourself the challenge to smile at 1 girl. That's it. You can run away straight after if you really want, but all you have to push yourself to do, is to smile at a single girl.

Then the next day, after your success of smiling at 1 girl, push yourself to smile at 2 girls, and continue to build your progress every day. Once you're comfortable smiling at girls, set yourself a challenge to say "Hi" to one, and then to hold a full conversation, then to ask one out! You can take big fears and goals and break them down into small steps that you work on every day.

Practicing exposing yourself to what you fear will help you quickly become used to it. Eventually, you'll develop a sense than doing things that make you feel anxious doesn't mean you have to avoid them.

AFTERWORD

Hopefully at least one of these strategies will help you to alleviate or completely overcome you Social Anxiety. If you find one of them has had a positive impact, continue that practice and maybe try one of the others in conjunction with it.

Make a point of writing down the results for each technique as this will help you figure out what worked for you, and what didn't.

One of the biggest points to bear in mind with any sort of life change is that these things can take time, so don't feel stressed out if some don't feel like they're working. Some of these techniques will likely deliver a positive effect from their first application, but others take time, so pick one and stick with it for a couple of weeks to reap the benefits!

Medication For Social Anxiety Disorder

Many psychologists agree that using medication, especially over the long-term, is an unsuitable way of dealing with Social Anxiety. As such, before resorting to medication, it's prudent to first explore non-pharmaceutical methods of relieving Social Anxiety. As mentioned earlier, the disorder is an illusion which can be overcome by changing your pattern of thinking. Medication may or may not complement various strategies for managing Social Anxiety.

Below are major types of medications that are typically utilized when treating Social Anxiety Disorder:

- Anti-anxiety medications
- Antidepressants
- Beta-blockers
- Benzodiazepines

We'll explore each of these and their associated pro's and con's below:

Anti-anxiety medications

These are powerful drugs that work to reduce anxiety rapidly after ingestion; however, these medications should never be taken for a long period as a tolerance is developed quickly. This caused the user to require higher and higher doses to get the same effect.

Unfortunately, this cycle commonly leads users to become addicts. Because of this, doctors usually prescribe anti-anxiety medications only for a short period.

The most common class of anti-anxiety drugs is Benzodiazepines. This class of drugs has a strong sedative effect which makes them unpopular among sufferers of Social Anxiety Disorder who want to maintain mental sharpness (or awakeness).

Antidepressants (Selective Serotonin Reuptake Inhibitor (SSRIs))

Antidepressants have been used for decades and are most commonly used to treat complications related to stress and depression. They can be very helpful for the symptoms of Social Anxiety Disorder.

Quite the opposite of most anti-anxiety medicines, antidepressants can take a few days to start working.

They also have many, sell documented, adverse side effects such as headaches, nausea, and difficulty sleeping. Some side effects are rare, especially if the dose starts off low and is gradually increased over time, but if these are drugs that you have been prescribed, it's important to tell your doctor about any side effects and, if necessary, work with your physician to try other medications.

Beta-blockers

These drugs can help to reduce the physical symptoms of anxiety. As discussed previously, the physical symptoms that are exhibited when a person has Social Anxiety Disorder, such as increased heart rate, trembling, and sweating, among others. All of these physical symptoms can be improved by use of a prescription of beta-blockers. Beta-blockers are currently the most common medication prescribed for performance anxiety.

Your doctor will determine the best medication and dose after a comprehensive diagnosis. People suffering with Social Anxiety Disorder who are prescribed these medications are likely to achieve optimal results when these medications are combined with other psychotherapies. Successful treatment depends on your ability to adapt to the changes brought about by either of these two methods.

However, it's worth noting that both psychotherapy and medication may take some time to work. A healthy lifestyle also helps combat Social Anxiety Disorder, so a focus on getting enough sleep, minimizing alcohol consumption, and eating a healthy diet. Most importantly, remember you can always turn to family and friends whom you trust for support when you need it.

FULLY RECOVERING

*W*hen you start out on your journey of recover from Social Anxiety Disorder, it may feel as if there is no end in site. Unfortunately, this feeling is all to common as many people who suffer with some form or another of Social Anxiety Disorder choose to take their own lives. This is a sad fact but, hopefully, one we can work to improve as more awareness of causes and treatments spreads.

I hope that with everything you've read in this book, you now feel better equipped to not only deal with the symptoms of Social Anxiety Order on a day-to-day basis, but also, that you do see a positive end in site - a day when you are fully recovered.

. . .

How Will I Know When I've Fully Recovered?

Fully recovering is a great achievement for anyone who has suffered Social Anxiety Disorder. For many people, once they realized they have achieved this milestone, it feels like a chance to enjoy a brand-new, positive and fulfilling life. Being able to live without being constantly overwhelmed with anxiety is incredibly freeing, especially when it has previously claimed so much for your existence. So, how will you know that you have fully recovered?

Here are some of the major signs that you have completely conquered you Social Anxiety Disorder:

You're able to attend social events

Weddings, church services, public lectures, and birthday parties are examples of the most commonly avoided social events for those suffering with Social Anxiety Disorder. Feeling comfortable at any social event is a sign of conquering anxiety and, whilst enduring a whole day among people may feel quite challenging and unpleasant the first few times, quickly you'll notice it starts to feel normal.

You don't concentrate on other people's judgments and thoughts

Not worrying about people's gossip is also a sign of full recovery. When you find your mind is naturally focusing on the more positive aspects of life, you'll notice you're more easily able to move on from upset.

You're social and easily converse with others

Not feeling shy in front of people is the key sign of a major improvement when overcoming Social Anxiety Disorder. Taking any chance to talk with new people can really help you gain confidence. One day you'll find yourself in the middle of a conversation with a group of friends and realise that you don't feel anxious or worried about anything. It's an amazing feeling and one of the most empowering moments in someone's life!

• • •

Public speaking

If you start feeling comfortable during public speaking, this is a sure sign of recovery; but still bear in mind that stage fright at the beginning of your presentation is absolutely normal. Provided the anxiousness you feel before public speaking isn't overwhelming and incapacitating, it should not be treated as a symptom of Social Anxiety Disorder and you can feel confident you are free of the disorder.

You're not constantly stressing about what *"might"* happen

Appreciating and internalising the belief that you can never change the outcome of certain future events is a major improvement. Paying attention to how you can influence future events by making better decisions is a great mind-set shift on the road to recovery from the disorder.

An absence of physical symptoms when faced with fear

If you find you are not sweating, trembling, or

noticing any of the other physical symptoms you've been used to when Social Anxiety kicked in, this is a clear indication your subconscious has internalised your new beliefs and is no longer causing your body to kick into the fight-or-flight response.

I really enjoyed my time with John. He shared everything while I sat and listened. Most of the things he mentioned were the normal feelings and worries every man has before starting a family. His major fear was starting a family and being unable to sustain them financially. For John, this feeling might have been further pronounced due to Mary's family's wealth. Since he felt like his salary wasn't enough to make Mary as comfortable as she would be in her father's house.

In order to understand John's situation better, I asked him a series of personal questions which he answered honestly. Being honest with your counselor is vital and has a big impact on how your problems are addressed. It also ensures that the solutions you receive are more personalized and viable for you to implement.

Intense anxiety about the future was a major blow to

John's confidence. He believed that Mary's parents would reject his proposal to marry their daughter and, therefore, he hadn't worked up the courage to do so. Once he worked through this limiting belief and realised the "rejection" was only an illusion of his mind, he began to start focusing on all of the positives in his relationship with Mary's parents.

John told me that he had a great relationship with her parents and that they always welcomed him warmly. Not once did they show any signs that they might disapprove of their relationship.

I advised John to dare himself to try what he deemed impossible. Let Mary's parents know his intention and propose to her! I'm pleased to say, John took the plunge to push his boundaries and now he and Mary are happily married with their first child on the way. After all his fears, John decided to push his boundaries and expand what he thought was possible!

RESOLUTIONS

*I*rrational thinking and negative self-talk is common for everyone, not just for people suffering from Social Anxiety Disorder. The easiest way to ensure you don't fall into this trap is of course to practice focusing on the positive aspects of your life, and frame them as resolutions to your perceived problems.

In order to maintain your positive outlook, make a list of your fears and come up with a viable resolution to each of them. Dare yourself to try what seems impossible.

Make a list of resolutions

. . .

In order to make a full recovery, try comminng up with a list of resolutions. Challenge yourself by listing things that you want to engage in more often.

The resolutions should be simple, logical, and, most importantly, achievable. You can choose to share the resolutions with your partner, friend, or a relative in order for them to keep you accountable and on-track. This way, you'll have someone to remind you about the resolutions and your chances of going astray will be massively reduced. Moreover, this can practice can go a long way to helping you evaluate the effectiveness of your resolutions.

To get you started, here are a few examples of some practical resolutions that may help you achieve and maintain a full recovery from Social Anxiety Disorder:

1. I will continually acquire more facts about Social Anxiety Disorder and the different ways to overcome it. This knowledge will give me power.
2. I will reflect more on the effects of Social

Anxiety on my health and social life and be ready to look for solutions.

3. I will look for new approaches to solve the disorder and create a gradual recovery procedure.

4. I will, at times, push my limits to provoke my fears. I will rank my fears to help me experiment with how effectively I can handle them.

5. I will make a list of ways that help reduce Social Anxiety and follow them to the letter.

6. I will be persistent in pursuing activities from my list, one at a time, sticking to the time limits and not giving up.

7. I will drive away some anxiety by focusing on what is going according to my plans. Dwelling on failures, misery, and setbacks will become a thing of the past.

8. I will use affirmations to overcome my Social Anxiety Disorder. I will create mottos that will help me move away from anxiety.

9. I will find some online reading materials, or even write my own, about improving self-esteem and overcoming Social Anxiety Disorder.

10. I will be social with others because there is a healing effect in human interactions.

11. I will be patient with myself as I work to overcome Social Anxiety Disorder.
12. I will be positive-minded and believe that I am stronger than anxiety.
13. I will be my own friend and I won't speak negatively about myself.
14. I won't fear meeting and talking to strangers and, instead, will make more friends from new people.
15. I will embrace the solutions as they are presented to me by a professional.

These resolutions are meant to guide you in making your own. Create a list of resolutions that will help you get better and give this disorder the boot!

ABOUT THE AUTHOR

Edward Jones was a normal guy, living a normal life. Then, over the course of a few months, his mental health started to deteriorate while anxiety, panic attacks and depression took over his life.

These problems steadily progressed and got worse and worse. Nothing was helping. he spoke to my doctor (who wanted to put him on drugs), but he made the decision that he wasn't going to go down that route. At his worst point, he could barely leave his room without feeling massive anxiety or succumbing to panic attacks.

It was then he decided to fix myself, no matter what.

That decision lead him down the path of researching and trying some of the most effective ways to control and eliminate anxiety, panic attacks and depression. It was a slow road to recovery, but it's been worth every second of it. He has his life back and now, he's happier than he's ever been!

Once he figured out what worked for him, Ed felt compelled to share his newfound knowledge and help as many others in the same situation as he could.

He always found that the most powerful thing can sometimes be knowing that someone else has gone through what you're going through, and that there is a solution.

He's been there, he feels your pain and he would love to help you get your life back!